LOOK INTO SPACE

EVERYDAY ASTRONOMY

Jon Kirkwood

ALADDIN/WATTS
LONDON • SYDNEY

An Aladdin Book
© Aladdin Books Ltd 1998
Produced by
Aladdin Books Ltd
28 Percy Street
London W1P 0LD

First published in Great Britain
in 1998 by
Aladdin Books/Watts Books
96 Leonard Street
London EC2A 4RH

ISBN 0-7496-3382-4

Editor: Jon Richards

Design

David West • CHILDREN'S BOOK DESIGN

Designer: Simon Morse

Illustrator: Ian Thompson

Picture research: Brooks Krikler Research

Printed in Belgium

The author, Jon Kirkwood, is a freelance
author and editor who has written a
number of books for both adults and
children, mainly on astronomy.

CONTENTS

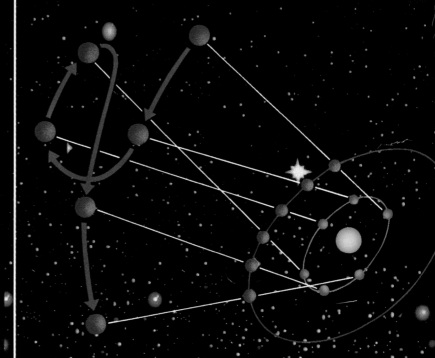

INTRODUCTION

Have you ever wondered what lies in space, beyond the comfort of the Earth? *Everyday Astronomy* **will take you on a tour of the heavens, starting back on Earth before heading out into the Solar System and off to the stars – all from the comfort of your armchair. Without knowing it, you encounter many astronomical principles every day, from the air you breathe in, to the Sun which lights the day and the gravity that keeps you firmly on the ground. All of these everyday things can be linked to the twinkling stars that glitter in the night sky above your head.**

EXCELLENT EXPERIMENTS

Wherever you see this symbol (*below*), you'll find an experiment which you can do. Just follow the easy-to-understand instructions, and the results will open your eyes to the wonders of space. Find out why objects fall back down to the ground and when it's best to see meteor showers.

STANDING ON THE GROUND

Perhaps the most important force in the universe is gravity. Without gravity, there would be nothing to hold you to the ground. Gravity is a force that attracts things to each other. Any object that has mass attracts any other object that has mass. The more massive the object, the more it attracts other objects. In space, gravity holds the universe together, keeping planets going around stars and holding stars together in clumps called galaxies.

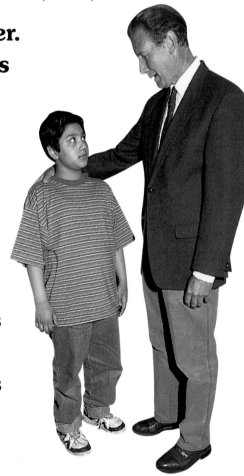

A person's weight depends upon how large his or her body is and how massive the planet is that he or she is standing on. On the Earth, a larger person will weigh more than a smaller person (below).

WHAT GOES UP...

Try throwing a ball up as hard as you can. It may fly up a few metres, but it will always come back down again (*left*). This is because of the Earth's gravitational force. The Earth is a very massive body and therefore has a strong force of gravity. When you throw the ball up, this strong attractive force pulls on the ball while it is rising through the air, slowing it down all the time. Eventually, the ball stops going up and the force then pulls it back down to the ground.

ROUND AND AROUND

Because it feels the same all the time, you generally don't notice the force of the Earth's gravity. But there are things that can make it feel as if gravity is changing. The aerobatics of a fighter aircraft or the movement of a rollercoaster ride at a theme park (*above*) are examples of these. They can make people feel as if the gravitational force is changing as they feel themselves become lighter or heavier.

FOR THE DROP

The force of gravity from the Earth's mass works equally on all objects at the Earth's surface, no matter what size they are. Take a small pebble and a larger stone and drop them from the same height at the same time. They will both hit a level surface at the same time. The force acts the same on the small stone as it does on the large one, moving them faster and faster toward the ground at the same rate.

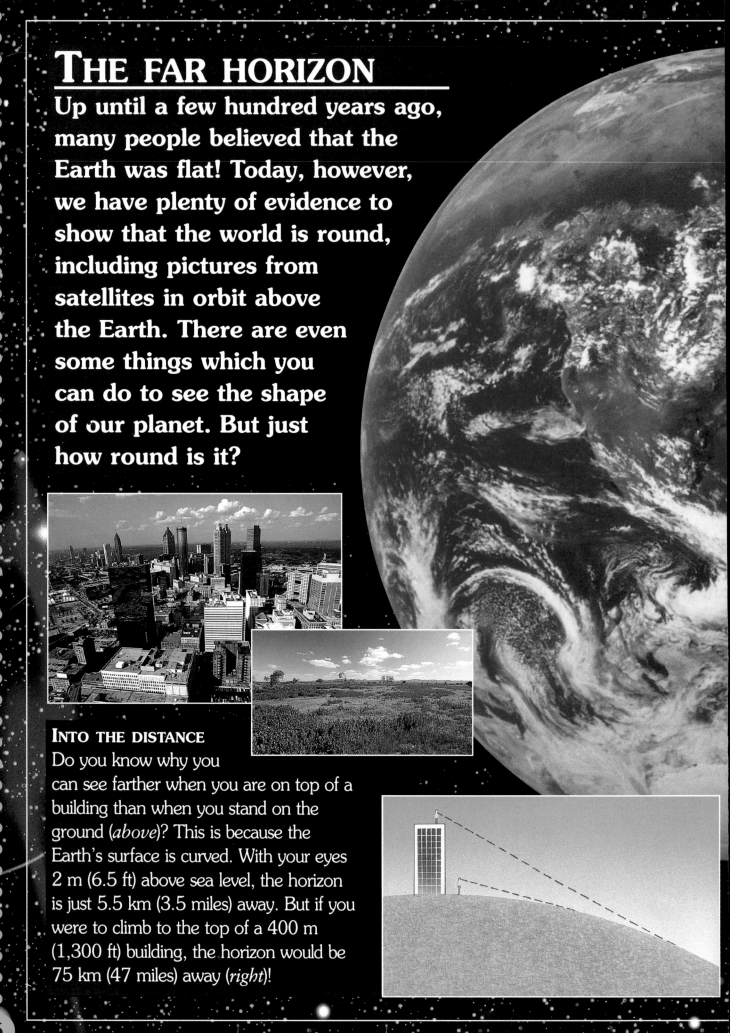

THE FAR HORIZON

Up until a few hundred years ago, many people believed that the Earth was flat! Today, however, we have plenty of evidence to show that the world is round, including pictures from satellites in orbit above the Earth. There are even some things which you can do to see the shape of our planet. But just how round is it?

INTO THE DISTANCE

Do you know why you can see farther when you are on top of a building than when you stand on the ground (*above*)? This is because the Earth's surface is curved. With your eyes 2 m (6.5 ft) above sea level, the horizon is just 5.5 km (3.5 miles) away. But if you were to climb to the top of a 400 m (1,300 ft) building, the horizon would be 75 km (47 miles) away (*right*)!

SQUASHED GLOBE

The Earth is not completely round! Measurements taken show that it bulges a bit at the equator. It is 42 km (26 miles) less from pole to pole than it is across the equator (*right*).

HUMBER ESTUARY BRIDGE

Because the Earth is round, objects set up at right angles to the ground will not be parallel to each other. Even the sides of tall buildings which are next to each other and might seem to be parallel are, in fact, at a slight angle to each other, albeit a tiny angle. This is not really obvious and it is only with tall structures some way apart that the angle becomes even detectable. For example, the towers of the Humber Estuary Bridge in the UK (*below*) are 1.4 km (0.9 miles) apart. The distance between their bases is 3.6 cm (1.4 in) less than the distance between their tops.

From this photo of the Earth (above) you can only see Africa and part of the Indian Ocean. If the Earth were flat you would be able to see the entire planet!

THE AIR WE BREATHE

The atmosphere is a layer of air that sits around the Earth and stretches upward into space. You can't see it, but it's all around you. You can feel it when you take a deep breath and blow out hard onto your hand in front of your face. This invisible mixture of gases is made up of tiny particles, some of which are vital to keeping you alive.

Look into a clear sky and it will appear blue (left). This is because the tiny air particles scatter the blue light in sunlight, and it is this blue light which you see.

THE HAZY HORIZON

When the Sun is very low in the sky, look at the horizon (never look directly at the Sun as this will cause eye damage) and you'll see the air is darker at the horizon and may be redder (*right*). The darkness is caused by dust and smoke in the air. The redness is caused by the fact that the Sun's light has to pass through more of the atmosphere when it is lower in the sky.

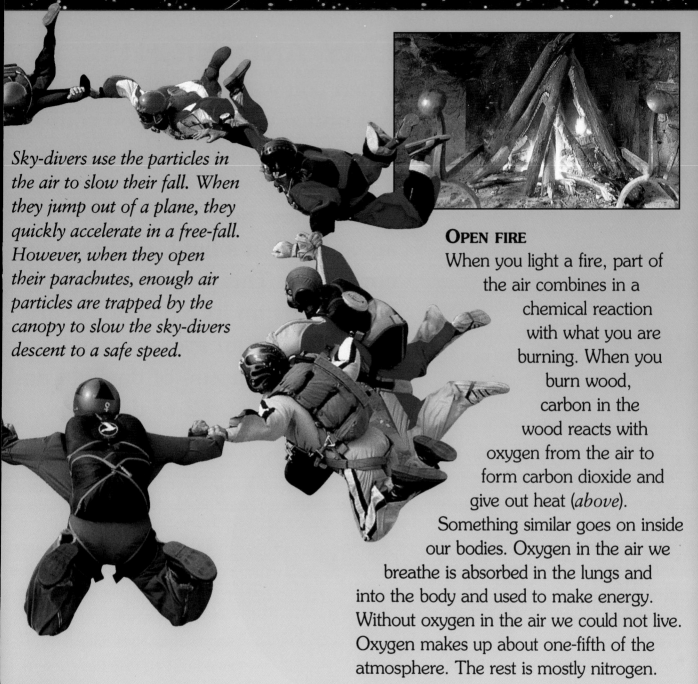

Sky-divers use the particles in the air to slow their fall. When they jump out of a plane, they quickly accelerate in a free-fall. However, when they open their parachutes, enough air particles are trapped by the canopy to slow the sky-divers descent to a safe speed.

OPEN FIRE

When you light a fire, part of the air combines in a chemical reaction with what you are burning. When you burn wood, carbon in the wood reacts with oxygen from the air to form carbon dioxide and give out heat (*above*). Something similar goes on inside our bodies. Oxygen in the air we breathe is absorbed in the lungs and into the body and used to make energy. Without oxygen in the air we could not live. Oxygen makes up about one-fifth of the atmosphere. The rest is mostly nitrogen.

CLOUDS

On most days you can see clouds in the sky (*right*). They are formed from water that has evaporated from rivers, lakes and the sea as well as damp soil and plants. This water vapour cools as it rises through the air. When it has cooled enough, it forms into the tiny droplets of water which make up the clouds. Water vapour in the air can also make things seem hazy when you look at them over a long distance.

Sun

Earth

DAY AND NIGHT

When you wake up, the first thing you notice when you open your eyes is whether it is dark or light. If it's dark you can be certain that within a few hours it will get light again and if it's light, darkness is not far off. This is because the Earth spins on its axis once every 24 hours. So an average day has 12 hours of daylight and 12 of darkness.

The Sun is much bigger than the Earth (left). While the Earth is 12,756 km (7,923 miles) across, the Sun is about 1,392,000 km (864,596 miles) in diameter, making it nearly 110 times wider than the Earth. Even so, the Sun is only able to provide heat and light to one side of the Earth at any one time. So, one half of the Earth will be light and the other dark (right).

SUNNY DAY

If the Sun is observed during the course of a day it seems to move across the sky. Take a picture of it every hour and you get a series of images with it spaced out equally (*below left*). The equal spacing comes from the fact that the Earth spins at a steady rate, neither speeding up or slowing down during a day.

Polar axis

SPIN SPEED

Because it is a sphere, the spinning Earth moves faster at the Equator than nearer the poles (*left*). At the Equator, the Earth's spin speed is about 1,600 km/h (994 mph), while at the poles it is almost zero. This has no real effect on people at these different latitudes, but rockets take advantage of the faster speed at the equator to get a boost into space. The extra spin speed at the Equator means they have to burn less fuel to get into orbit. The European Space Agency's Ariane rockets, for instance, are launched from French Guiana, near the Equator (*below*).

Surface moves faster at the equator.

WIND IN A SPIN

One effect of the Earth's rotation is to make weather systems spiral. For example, as air moves northward away from the equator, the Earth's rotation will push the air to the east. Once it starts to curve, it starts spiralling, especially if the weather is violent as in a hurricane (*below*).

Ariane V rocket blasts clear of its launch pad in French Guiana.

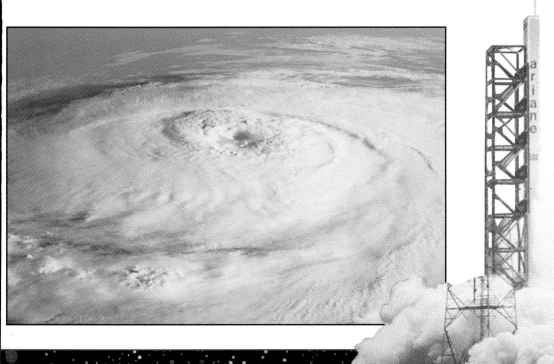

CHANGING SEASONS

During each year, the weather changes and the countryside changes with it. It gets colder in the winter and many plants die or sleep through the chilly months. After this, the weather gets warmer and plants re-grow through spring and into summer, before dying off again as the weather cools off during autumn and back again into the cold of winter. The cycle of the seasons is caused by the Earth's path, or orbit, around the Sun. This varies the amount of energy that the surface receives from our nearest star.

Tree in winter

Tree in spring

Tree in summer

Tree in autumn

THE LONG AND THE SHORT OF IT

Over the course of the year, watch how your shadow changes at the same time of the day. In summer, it will be very short. That is because the Sun is high in the sky. But in winter, your shadow will be very long as the Sun does not get very high in the sky during this season (*below*).

Summer shadow

Winter shadow

TILTING PLANET

The changes of the seasons are caused because the Earth is tilted at an angle in its orbit around the Sun (23.5° to be precise!). At one point in its orbit, the northern half of the planet will be tilted towards the Sun and the southern half away. At this point, the northern half will receive more energy from the Sun than the southern half, making it summer in the north and winter in the south (right). Six months later, the opposite will be true. The southern half will be tilted towards the Sun and the northern half away from it (below).

Summer in the north

Winter in the south

Autumn in the north, spring in the south

Winter in the north, summer in the south

Sun

Spring in the north, autumn in the south

Summer in the north, winter in the south

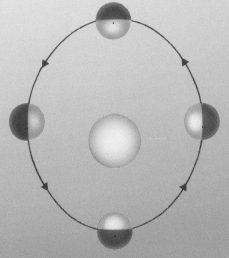

The Earth's elliptical orbit

SQUASHED ORBIT

The Earth's orbit round the Sun is not a perfect circle, it is in a squashed circle called an ellipse (*left*). In an elliptical orbit, the object around which a body orbits is always closer to one end of the ellipse. As a result, the Earth gets closer to the Sun for part of the year. This coincides with the time when the southern hemisphere is tilted toward the Sun. Because it is closer to the Sun at this time, the southern half of the Earth gets more energy from the Sun during its summer than the northern half does during its summer.

TELLING TIME

Our notion of time comes from what we experience of the world around us. The most obvious change in the everyday world that marks the passage of time is the regular day-night cycle (*see* pages 10-11). However, to get a more accurate impression of time, we have broken a day down into hours, minutes and seconds. Today, we tell the time using very sophisticated equipment which is extremely accurate.

TIME SHADOW

Before watches and clocks, people used the position of the Sun to tell the time. An angled stick, called a gnomon, would cast a shadow on the ground. This shadow would move as the Sun moved across the sky. This device is called a sundial (*below*). Try to make your own sundial. Push a stick into the ground and mark on the ground where the stick's shadow points to at every hour.

A long-exposure photo of the night sky shows that stars appear to go in circles as the Earth spins (above). A day is defined by the time it takes for a star to travel a complete circle around the sky.

-12 -10 -8 -6 -4 -2 0 +2 +4 +6 +8 +10 +12

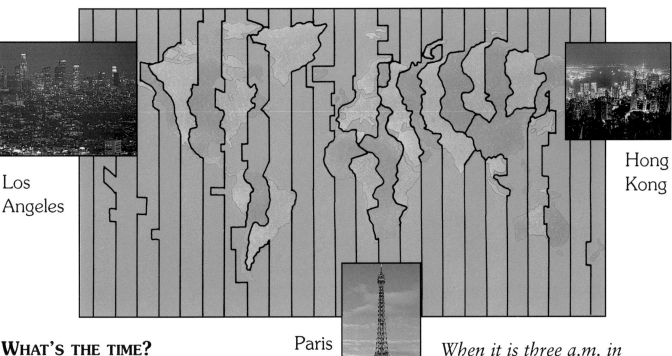

Los Angeles

Hong Kong

Paris

WHAT'S THE TIME?

Because only half of the Earth is in sunlight, it can be daylight in one city and night-time in another on the other side of the world. It would be impractical for every place on Earth to keep the same time. As such, the Earth is divided into bands or time zones, each with its own local time (*above*). This system was devised around an imaginary line which runs through Greenwich, London.

When it is three a.m. in Los Angeles, it is noon in Paris and seven p.m. in Hong Kong.

TIME THROUGH THE AGES

Many ancient cultures built structures that could measure the regular cycles of the Sun and stars. The Aztecs used a massive calendar stone (*right*) to measure what they believed were the five cycles of world creation. They also used a solar calendar of 365 days and a sacred calendar of 260 days. The combination of these led to cycles of 52 years. At Stonehenge in Wiltshire, England (*left*), the huge standing stones mark several regular cycles, including the place where the Sun rises at midsummer. Building of these standing stones began around 1800 BC.

Stonehenge

THE SPECTRUM

Look up in the sky at night and you can see the stars. This is because you can see the visible light which the stars give out. But visible light forms a small part of the energy band called the electromagnetic spectrum. This includes invisible rays, such as radio waves, x-rays and gamma rays.

OVER THE RAINBOW
The range of colours of visible light can be seen in all its glory when a rainbow forms (left). This is sunlight broken into its component colours: red, orange, yellow, green, blue, indigo and violet. Water droplets in the air from rain act like tiny prisms to split the light up into its different colours.

LOW-ENERGY WAVES
Beyond the red end of the spectrum are the low-energy waves. With these, the peaks of each wave of energy are further apart than those of high-energy waves. These low-energy waves include infra-red radiation, microwaves and radio waves. While microwaves and infra-red radiation are blocked by the Earth's atmosphere, radio waves can travel through it.

Astronomers can detect radio waves from space using large metal dishes called radio telescopes (left).

WARMTH OF THE SUN

Lie out in the Sun too long and you might burn if you don't wear sun-protection products (*below*). This burn comes from ultraviolet radiation produced by the Sun. Astronomers can study ultraviolet radiation to discover more about what goes on deep inside stars.

SNAP HAPPY

Visible light can be recorded on film to make photographs (*right*). Other forms of electromagnetic radiation can be made into pictures as well. For instance, satellites in orbit can detect various forms of radiation using equipment that is sensitive to them, including x-rays, infra-red radiation and gamma rays. Computers can then use this data to form 'pictures' from these invisible rays.

THE RANGE OF WAVES

The whole range of the electromagnetic spectrum goes from radio waves through microwaves and infra-red. Then comes visible light after which is ultraviolet, then x-rays and finally gamma rays.

SEEING INSIDE

X-rays are from the high-energy part of the electromagnetic spectrum. They have a very short distance between the peaks of their energy waves and can pass right through you! Doctors use x-rays to look into your body (*left*). In space, x-rays are given off by very energetic objects, such as clouds of gas whirling around black holes.

THE COMPASS

There's a huge and powerful force field surrounding our planet. But you can't see it and you can't feel it. However, there are a number of clues to its existence. These include the strange lights that can sometimes be seen in the night sky near the North and South Poles. The force field has also been used by travellers and explorers for centuries to help them find their way. This force field is called the Earth's magnetic field.

AHOY THERE

Compasses (*above*), in one form or another, have been around for 4,500 years! Some 800 years ago, European and Chinese seamen would use a magnetic stone, called a lodestone, which pointed north.

NIGHT LIGHT

The northern and southern lights (*above*) are another consequence of Earth having a magnetic field. At the North and South Poles, the solar wind – a stream of charged particles shot out by the Sun – is channelled by the magnetic field until they get near to the Earth (*right*). Here, they interact with the air particles to make multi-coloured lights in the sky.

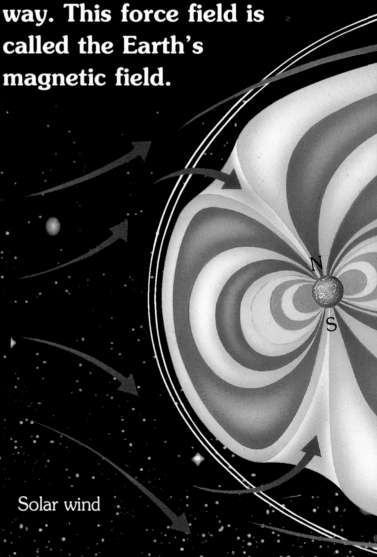

N

S

Solar wind

FIND YOUR WAY

If you have a compass (*left*) and a map, you can always get a rough idea of where you are. Even without a map, a compass will point north so that you can work out which direction you have to go (*right*).

However, the north the compass points to is not true north, but a spot about 11.5 degrees south from it, called the magnetic north pole. This is because the Earth's magnetic field does not line up with its axis of rotation.

OUR INVISIBLE FORCE FIELD

The Earth's magnetic field is much bigger than the Earth itself. It stretches out above, below, in front of, and behind our planet (*below*).

Magnetic field

TIME FOR A DIP

As well as running north/south, the lines of force of the Earth's magnetic field emerge from the ground at an angle. You can see this using a compass. First point the compass north. Turn the compass on its side (*below*) and the needle should point into the ground at an angle. This angle depends upon where you are on the Earth. For example, the further you are from the equator, the steeper the angle your compass points into the ground.

CHANGING MOON

Much of the time you can see the Moon in the night sky. But the Moon, unlike the Sun, seems to change in shape over the course of a few days. It goes from being a thin silver sliver to a round shining ball and back over the course of about four weeks. These apparent changes in its shape are called phases.

Crescent Moon

First quarter

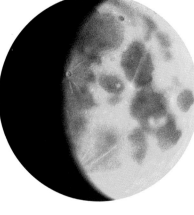

Gibbous Moon

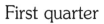

Full Moon

ROUND AND AROUND

The Moon does not shine! What we see at night is light from the Sun that is reflected off the Moon's surface. When the Moon is between us and the Sun, the Moon appears to disappear – what we call a new moon. As the Moon moves around the Earth every 28 days, the amount we see changes into a thin crescent moon (*above*), then a fuller, gibbous moon to a point where we can see all of its illuminated surface – what we call a full moon (*right*).

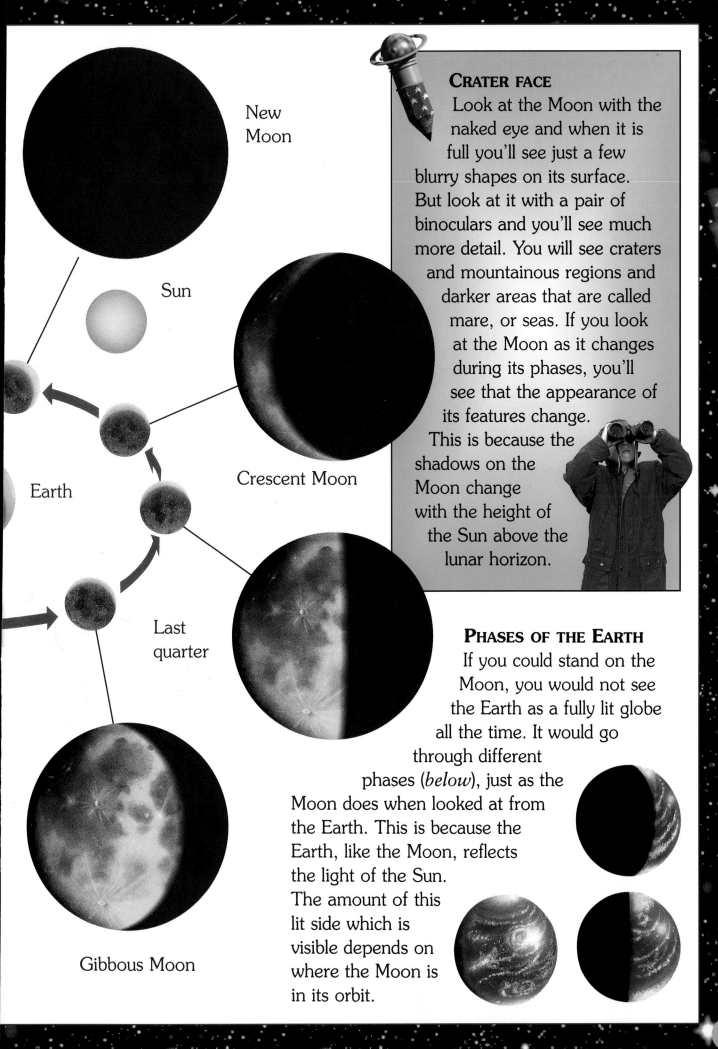

New
Moon

Sun

Earth

Crescent Moon

Last
quarter

Gibbous Moon

CRATER FACE

Look at the Moon with the
naked eye and when it is
full you'll see just a few
blurry shapes on its surface.
But look at it with a pair of
binoculars and you'll see much
more detail. You will see craters
and mountainous regions and
darker areas that are called
mare, or seas. If you look
at the Moon as it changes
during its phases, you'll
see that the appearance of
its features change.
This is because the
shadows on the
Moon change
with the height of
the Sun above the
lunar horizon.

PHASES OF THE EARTH

If you could stand on the
Moon, you would not see
the Earth as a fully lit globe
all the time. It would go
through different
phases (*below*), just as the
Moon does when looked at from
the Earth. This is because the
Earth, like the Moon, reflects
the light of the Sun.
The amount of this
lit side which is
visible depends on
where the Moon is
in its orbit.

VANISHING SUN, VANISHING MOON

Because the Moon is much closer to the Earth than the Sun, it appears to be the same size even though the Sun is larger. When the Moon travels in front of the Sun, it can block it out completely. This is a solar eclipse. A lunar eclipse happens when the Earth passes between the Moon and the Sun, darkening the Moon with its shadow.

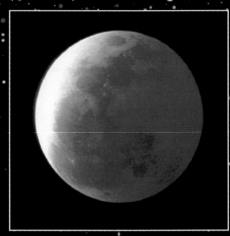

During some lunar eclipses the Moon can glow red (above). This is because red light is bent by the Earth's atmosphere onto the Moon.

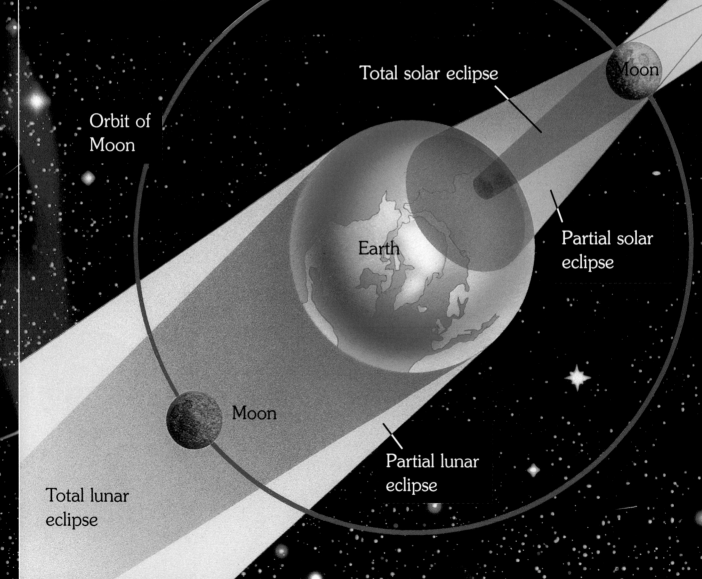

Total solar eclipse

Moon

Orbit of Moon

Earth

Partial solar eclipse

Moon

Partial lunar eclipse

Total lunar eclipse

SOLAR ECLIPSE

During a solar eclipse, the moon casts a cone-shaped shadow where a total eclipse occurs (*below*). Around this is a half-shaded area where partial eclipses occur.

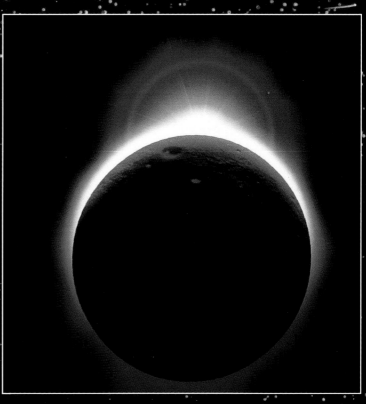

Sun

THE SWEEPING SHADOWS

When they do occur, solar eclipses do not cover a large area and do not last for very long. This is because the Moon travels quickly through its orbit and is far enough away from the Earth to cast only a small shadow, about 250 km (155 miles) wide. Below are the paths of the total eclipses for the next few years.

WHERE'S THE SUN GONE?

During a total eclipse, the sky goes dark and stars come out. Just before the Sun is fully covered, the edge of it shines out from behind the Moon (*above*).
WARNING: never look directly at the Sun, even during a total eclipse.

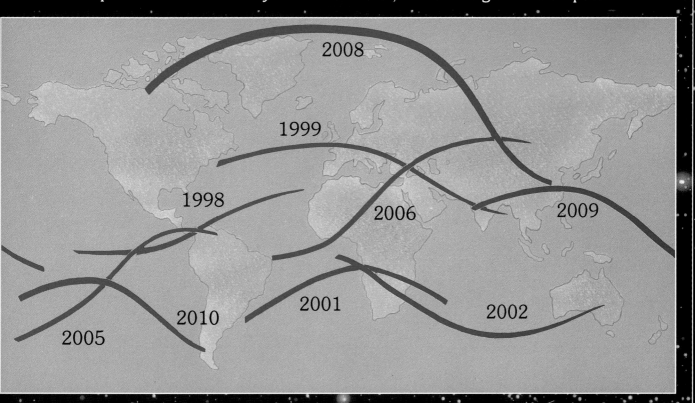

2008

1999

1998

2006

2009

2001

2002

2010

2005

TWINKLING STARS

Look up in the night sky when it's clear and dark and you'll see the stars. On a really clear night you can see thousands of them. If you study them hard enough you will notice that no two stars appear to be exactly the same. They will vary in brightness as well as twinkle slightly and even differ in colour.

This picture of the stars (above) *shows how they can vary greatly in brightness.*

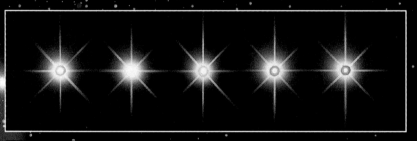

Hottest ⟶ Coolest

THE COLOUR OF HEAT

Stars come in different colours, depending on the temperature of their surface. For example, a red star is cooler than an orange star which is cooler than a yellow star (*above*).

Light from a star

WHY THEY TWINKLE

The light from a star passes more or less unhindered through space until it gets close to the Earth. However, just before it reaches the Earth's surface it has to pass through the atmosphere. As it passes through the air, the starlight can be bent off course by air particles and air currents. This makes the star appear to flicker, or twinkle, to someone on the ground (*left*).

Vega

Aldebaran

Our Sun

FROM SMALL TO BIG

Stars come in different sizes (*below*). Our star, the Sun, is not a very big star. Vega is a blue-white star that is several times wider than the Sun. Aldebaran is an orange-coloured star about 20 times bigger than the Sun. Betelgeuse is a giant red star, about 600 times as wide as our Sun.

Betelgeuse

THE SISTERS

Look in the northern sky during winter and you will see a little group of stars clustered together in the group of stars or constellation known as Taurus (*see* pages 26-27). This collection of stars is named the Pleiades or the Seven Sisters, although only six are easy to spot with the naked eye. These are a group of stars that have formed together in a star cluster. The brightest stars in the cluster are a brilliant blue. They are blue because they are burning very fiercely (*see left*), and fierce-burning stars do not live for long. This indicates that they were born a short time ago.

1

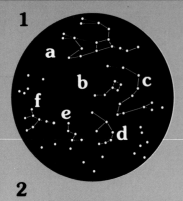

2

NAMING STARS

People have always made up stories about the stars, linking them into groups and naming them after characters. You can use these groups to divide the sky and find your way from star to star.

Star chart divisions

3

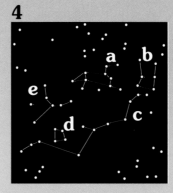

Map 1 (top)
a Ursa Major,
b Ursa Minor,
c Draco, d Cephus,
e Cassiopeia,
f Perseus

Map 2 (above)
a Andromeda,
b Pegasus,
c Cygnus, d Pisces,
e Aquarius,
f Capricornus

Map 3 (above)
a Hercules, b Boötes,
c Ophiucus,
d Aquila, e Libra,
f Scorpio,
g Sagittarius

Map 4 (below)
a Leo,
b Cancer,
c Hydra,
d Corvus, e Virgo

4

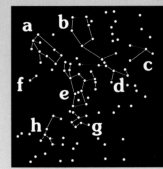

Map 5 (below)
a Gemini, b Auriga,
c Aries, d Taurus,
e Orion, f Canis
Minor, g Lepus,
h Canis Major

Map 6 (bottom)
a Hydrus, b Pavo,
c Ara, d Triangulum
Australe, e Octans,
f Musca, g Crux,
h Volans

5

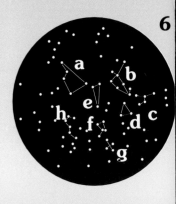

SEEING STARS

The groups that stars are divided into are called constellations. To show these clearly, we have divided the sky into six star charts (*above*). These show the major constellations, including the zodiac signs and Orion with his three-starred belt, his war club and his shield (*left*).

6

STAR POINTERS

You don't need highly detailed star maps to find your way around the night sky – the stars themselves will act as pointers. Take a look at the three star maps on this page. By using bright stars that come in easy-to-recognise patterns, you can make your way from star to star, finding some interesting points as you go. For example, the three stars in Orion's belt will point you towards the brightest star in the sky – Sirius (*below*).

THE POINTING HUNTER

Orion can be used to find Sirius (*right*). The three stars in his belt also point the way to the constellation Taurus. By using the star Rigel and the middle star of his belt you can find the star Castor in the constellation Gemini.

NORTHERN POINTERS

Seven stars form part of Ursa Major. These stars are called The Big Dipper or The Plough (*above*). The two stars on the right-hand edge will point the way to the Pole Star and also to Leo. It also points to the constellation Lynx and the bright star Arcturus.

SOUTHERN CROSS

The constellation Crux, which is also known as the Southern Cross, is easy to find in the sky above the southern hemisphere. It points toward the south celestial pole, the point directly above the Earth's South Pole (*left*). It also points towards the nearby constellation of Centaurus, and to the brightest star in that constellation, Alpha Centauri. Alpha Centauri is the second closest star to our own.

MOVING STARS

As well as the Sun, Moon and background stars, the sky has a few more objects in it that cannot help but catch your attention. These are the five bright, star-like objects that seem to wander about the sky, sometimes in the most bizarre ways. These wandering 'stars' are in fact some of the other planets of the Solar System.

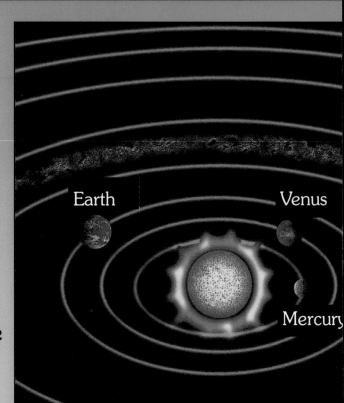

Earth

Venus

Mercury

The Solar System consists of nine major planets which orbit the Sun (above). There is also a band of small, rocky bodies, called the Asteroid Belt, which is found between the orbits of Mars and Jupiter. Of the planets, only five are visible with the naked eye. These are Mercury, Venus, Mars, Jupiter and Saturn. The other planets are too small or too far away to see without a telescope.

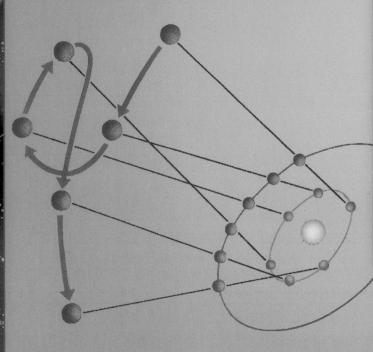

A time-lapse picture, showing the looping movement of Mars over a few months.

MEANDERING MARS

Mars appears to wander more than any other planet, as this image shows (*right*). The reasons for this are that it orbits the Sun more slowly than the Earth and its orbit is outside the Earth's. As a result, as the Earth catches up and overtakes it, Mars appears to double back on itself (*above*).

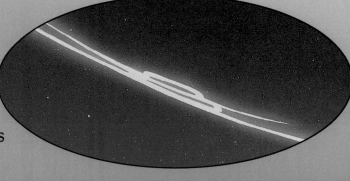

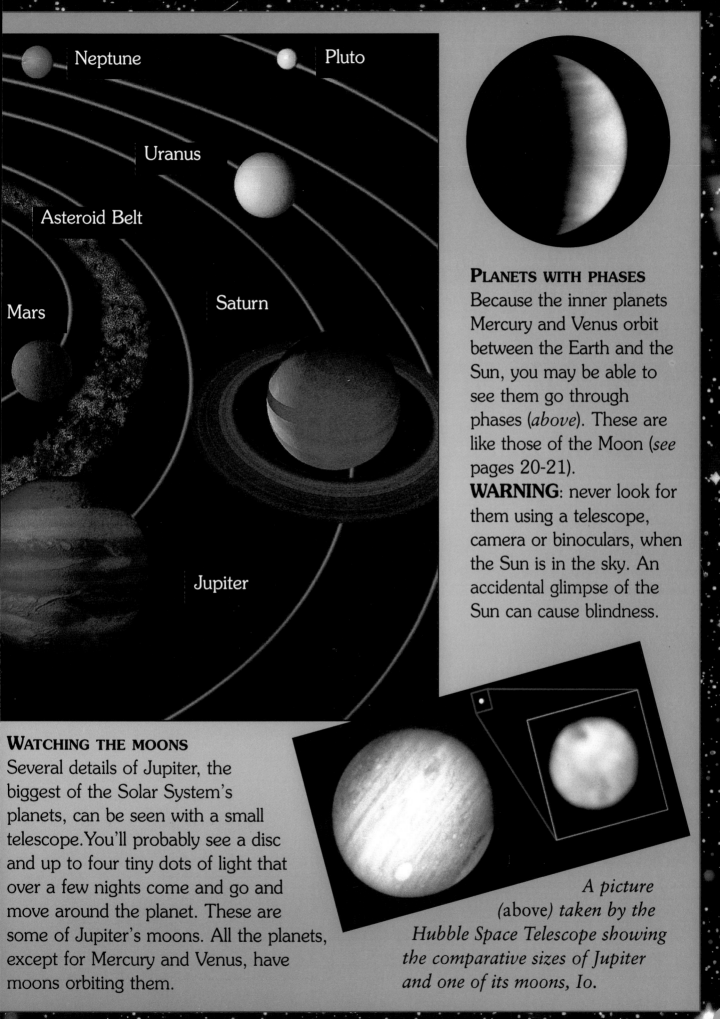

Neptune

Pluto

Uranus

Asteroid Belt

Mars

Saturn

Jupiter

Planets with phases

Because the inner planets Mercury and Venus orbit between the Earth and the Sun, you may be able to see them go through phases (*above*). These are like those of the Moon (*see* pages 20-21).

WARNING: never look for them using a telescope, camera or binoculars, when the Sun is in the sky. An accidental glimpse of the Sun can cause blindness.

Watching the moons

Several details of Jupiter, the biggest of the Solar System's planets, can be seen with a small telescope. You'll probably see a disc and up to four tiny dots of light that over a few nights come and go and move around the planet. These are some of Jupiter's moons. All the planets, except for Mercury and Venus, have moons orbiting them.

A picture (above) taken by the Hubble Space Telescope showing the comparative sizes of Jupiter and one of its moons, Io.

OCCASIONAL VISITORS

The space between the planets is far from empty. Orbiting the Sun are countless small bodies made up of rock and ice. Sometimes, these bodies pass close to the Earth and some even bump into its atmosphere leaving fiery trails that flare up and disappear in a few seconds. A few actually survive this and hit the Earth, sometimes leaving huge scars. Other icy bodies can light up the night sky, trailing huge glowing tails that you can see for several weeks.

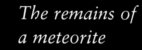

The remains of a meteorite

FIERY TAILS

The tails of some comets can be very visible in the night sky. Comet Hale-Bopp passed the Earth in 1997. This picture (*above*) shows just how bright its tails were. Streaming straight behind the comet's nucleus is a bluish tail made from gas. The brighter tail which points off to the right is made up of dust thrown off by the nucleus as it approaches the Sun.

DEEP IMPACT

Not every piece of matter burns up when it hits the Earth's atmosphere. Larger chunks can slam into the Earth with tremendous force, creating craters, like this one in Arizona, USA (*right*). When a piece of matter hits the Earth's surface it is called a meteorite. Large meteorites hit the Earth once every 10,000 years!

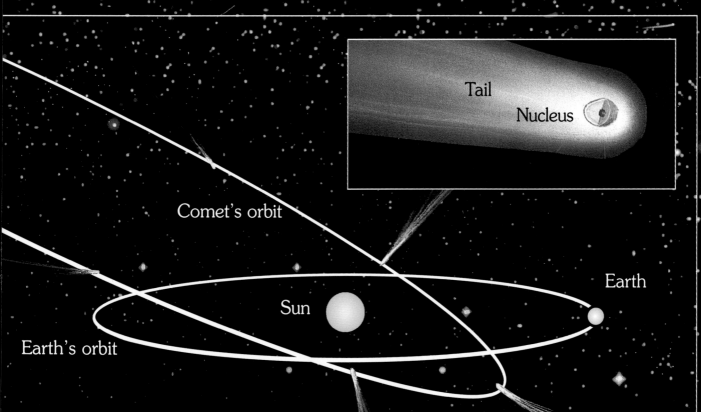

Tail

Nucleus

Comet's orbit

Earth

Sun

Earth's orbit

VISITORS FROM AFAR

Comets are basically dirty snow-balls that orbit the Sun in a long, path called an ellipse (*above*). When they come close to the Sun, radiation from the Sun boils off the outer layers of the comet which stream out in front of the comet to form a coma (*top*) before being blown back by the solar wind, a stream of particles sent out by the Sun, to form the tails. As such, the comet's tails always point away from the Sun and, at their longest, they can stretch for nearly 160 million km (100 million miles)! Then, as the comet swings around the Sun and begins to move back out into space, its tail gets smaller and slowly disappears.

METEOR SHOWERS

At certain times of the year, the night sky lights up with streaks of light caused by tens and sometimes hundreds of meteors burning up in the atmosphere. These are called meteor showers and they occur when the Earth passes through a trail of comet debris. These storms occur at regular times during the year and are named after the constellation they appear in. The chart (*left*) lists some of them, their dates and how long they last.

DATES OF METEOR SHOWERS

Quadrantids – January 3, 5 nights

Lyrids – April 22, 5 nights

Delta Aquarids – July 29, 8 nights

Capricornids – July 30, 3 nights

Perseids – August 12, 6 nights

Draconids – October 9, 1 night

Orionids – October 21, 2 nights

Geminids – December 14, 4 nights

THE MILKY WAY

On a really clear night, away from the glare of street lights, you should be able to see a milky band of light stretching across the sky. This band is called the Milky Way. It is actually made up of billions and billions of stars. These are held together in an enormous group called a galaxy, which includes our Sun. What we see as the Milky Way is a side-on view of what is really a massive disc. This disc is so big that it would take a ray of light over 100,000 years to travel across it!

CLOUDS IN THE WAY

Unfortunately, the view we get of the Milky Way is spoiled by vast clouds of gas and dust that lie between us and the centre (*left*). Like clouds in our sky that block the light from stars in the night sky, these clouds stop the light from distant stars from reaching us. However, astronomers can 'see' through these clouds by using instruments that can detect invisible wavelengths, such as infra-red radiation (*see* pages 16-17).

OUR GALAXY

Our galaxy is shaped like a huge flattened spiral (*above*). At the centre is a massive bulge which astronomers believe contains an enormous black hole. There are also a series of arms which spiral out from the bulge. The whole galaxy is 100,000 light-years across (*see* pages 36-37) and about 10,000 light-years from top to bottom.

*Our Sun sits in one of the galaxy's huge spiral arms, called the Orion Arm (*above*).*

BLOCKING CLOUDS

The majority of the huge clouds of dust and gas which hide our view of the galaxy's centre are found in the spiral arms. These clouds are called dark nebulae because they absorb the light from stars behind them (*right*).

PEARLY PATCHES

As well as the blurred band of the Milky Way, there are other smudge-like patches in the night sky. They look very different from stars because, although they glow, they do not appear as a point of light as stars do. These smudges can be huge clouds of gas, such as the Orion Nebula (*right*). They may also be the remains of an exploding star or they could even be whole galaxies. Unfortunately, most of these pearly patches are too dim to see without a telescope, but you should still be able to spot a couple.

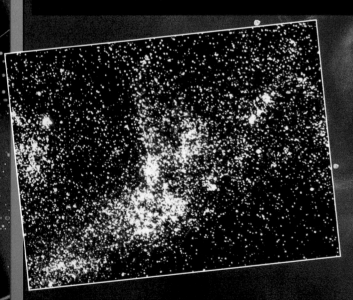

MAGELLANIC CLOUDS
In the southern skies observers can see two patches (*above*). These are two mini-galaxies close to our own and are called the Large and Small Magellanic Clouds.

GALACTIC SMUDGES

Some patches in the sky are actually huge galaxies (*left*) like our own Milky Way (*see* pages 32-33). They appear very small because they are millions of light years away (*see* pages 36-37). The nearest galaxy to our own can actually be seen without the aid of a telescope. The Andromeda galaxy is a small smudge which can be found in the constellation of the same name. It is over two million light years away, and is the most distant object that you can see with the naked eye.

The Orion Nebula (left) can be found just below the three stars of Orion's belt.

CLOUDS THAT NEVER RAIN

The space between stars is not completely empty. There are always traces of gas and dust, and sometimes these traces can become so dense as to form huge clouds which you can see. These clouds are called nebulae. They can glow with the light from stars, like the nebula in Orion (*right*), or they can block out starlight altogether, leaving massive black blobs (*see* pages 32-33). These nebulae are huge, some stretching over hundreds of light years. Other nebulae are much smaller. They are the remains of stars that have exploded leaving just an expanding shell of glowing gas, such as the Hour-glass Nebula (*above*).

HOW FAR AWAY?

Distances in space are huge. While it may seem a huge distance between the Earth and the Sun, this is tiny against the distances between stars. Conventional units such as kilometres become useless when talking about these enormous distances. Instead, astronomers use the distance that light can travel in a year – a light-year.

To get an idea of how fast light travels, measure the time between the moment you see a lightning flash and when you hear the thunder.

Earth

Moon

Sun

MOON

At 384,400 km (238,860 miles) distant, the Moon is the Earth's nearest neighbour in space. Light from the Moon takes nearly one and a half seconds to travel the distance between the Moon and the Earth (*above*).

SUN

Even though the Sun is our nearest star, it is still 150 million kilometres (93 million miles) away, about 375 times as far away from the Earth as the Moon is. The light that the Sun creates takes about eight minutes to travel from the Sun to us on Earth (*above*).

PLUTO

Pluto (*below*) is usually the farthest planet of the nine planets which make up the Solar System (because of Pluto's strange orbit, Neptune can sometimes be farther away!). It is about 40 times the distance between the Earth and the Sun. As such, it takes light about five and a half hours to cover the distance between the Earth and Pluto.

Pluto

PROXIMA CENTAURI

Proxima Centauri (*below*) is the nearest star to the Sun. It is about 41 million million km (25 million million miles) from us. To simplify this huge figure, we say that the star is just over four light-years away, because it takes light from it just over four years to reach us.

Proxima Centauri

ANDROMEDA GALAXY

The nearest galaxy to our own Milky Way is the Andromeda Galaxy (*see* page 35). The light from this distant object that is reaching us now actually left the Andromeda Galaxy over two million years ago!

Andromeda Galaxy

Communications satellite

SATELLITE TIME DELAY

The speed of light can actually be experienced when making a long-distance telephone call. The chances are that your telephone conversation will be transmitted as radio signals, which travel at the speed of light. These will be transmitted to satellites orbiting high above the Earth and then retransmitted back to the surface, perhaps several times (*right*). Even though these signals travel at the speed of light, the distance is so great that there will be a slight delay between you finishing talking and the signal arriving with your caller. There will also be a delay in any return messages.

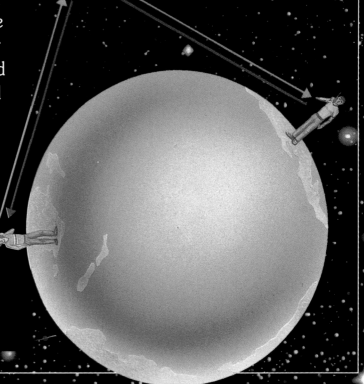

GLOSSARY

Asteroids
Small rocky objects, the greatest collection of which orbit the Sun in a band called the Asteroid Belt between Mars and Jupiter.

Atmosphere
The layer of gases which surround a planet. The atmosphere around Earth supplies us with the gases that keep us alive.

Black holes
The remains of massive stars that have exploded and collapsed in on themselves. The resulting gravity is so strong that not even light can escape.

Comets
Lumps of ice and dust that orbit around the Sun.

Compass
A device which can detect a planet's magnetic field using a magnetised needle.

Constellation
A collection of stars which have been grouped together in the night sky. Constellations are usually named after gods, heroes or animals.

Day
The length of time it takes for a planet to complete one rotation. An Earth day lasts 23.93 hours, while a day on Saturn lasts only 10.23 hours.

Eclipse
The total or partial disappearance of an object. This is caused by another object passing between it and an observer, or by its passing into a shadow.

Electromagnetic spectrum
The entire range of radiation, ranging from radio waves to gamma rays and including visible light, x-rays and infra-red radiation.

Equator
An imaginary line which runs around a planet at an equal distance from its two poles. It marks the planet's widest part.

Galaxy
An enormous cluster of stars. Each galaxy can contain many billions of stars. Galaxies are classified as spiral-shaped, elliptical or irregular. Our own galaxy is a spiral-shaped galaxy called the Milky Way.

Gravity
Every object in the universe has a force which attracts it to every other object. This force is called gravity. The larger or more dense the object, the greater its gravitational force. A large and very dense object, such as the Sun, will have a higher gravitational force than a smaller, less dense object, such as the Earth.

Light-years
Units used to measure distances in space. One light-year is the distance that a beam of light will travel in a year. This is equivalent to 9.6 million million km (5.9 million million miles).

Meteors
Objects which hit the Earth's atmosphere and burn up leaving a fiery trail which disappears after a few seconds. Objects which survive this and hit the Earth's surface are called meteorites.

Milky Way
The galaxy that contains our Sun. It is called the Milky Way because it appears as a milky band which runs across the night sky.

Moons
Small bodies that orbit around some of the major planets. The Earth has one moon, while Venus has none and Jupiter has at least 16!

Nebulae
Clouds of gas that float about in space. They may be thousands of light-years across. Many nebulae are the remains of stars thrown off during an explosion, or nova.

Orbit
The path of an object, such as a planet or a comet, around another object, such as a star.

Phases
The changes which an object appears to go through as it orbits another. These changes are caused by an observer only being able to see the lit part of an object.

Planets
Large objects which orbit around a star. These can be rocky planets such as the Earth, Venus or Mars, or gassy giant planets, such as Jupiter, Uranus or Saturn.

Pole
A point on a planet's surface around which the planet spins, or rotates.

Satellite
An object which goes around, or orbits another, larger object. Satellites can be natural, such as moons, or artificial, such as weather satellites.

Solar System
The group of major planets, including the Earth, and minor planets that orbit the Sun.

Stars
Objects which generate enormous amounts of heat and light. They do this by squashing together the gas particles which make them up, releasing huge amounts of energy.

Year
The length of time it takes for a planet to orbit its star. An Earth year is 365.25 days.

INDEX

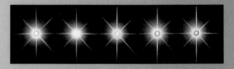